Tiger Talk
Get Into Science

Shape and Build

Leon Read

W
FRANKLIN WATTS
LONDON • SYDNEY

Contents

Look out for Tiger on the pages of this book. Sometimes he is hiding.

We use materials to make things.

I'm shaping this clay.

I'm building with these plastic blocks.

3

Stretchy, soft

Some materials are easy to shape.

We use these words to describe them:

- soft,
- bendy,
- stretchy,
- squashy,
- spongy,
- flexible.

What soft materials can you find?

Firm, tough

Some materials are
difficult to shape.

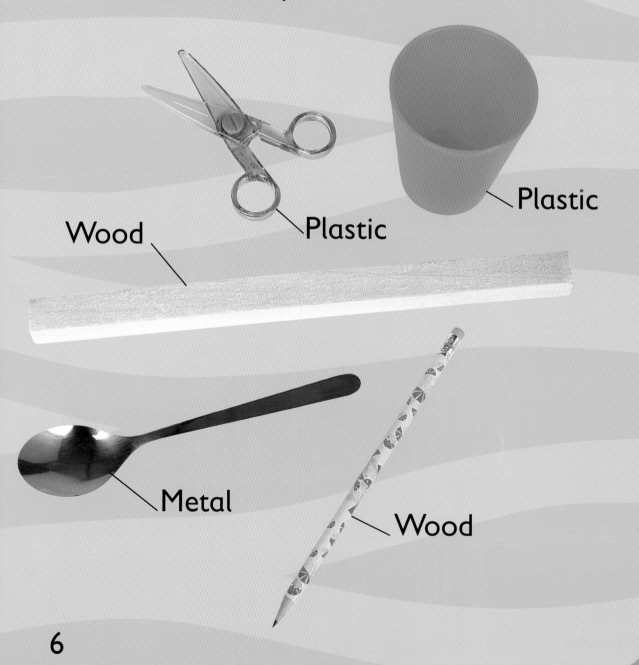

Plastic

Plastic

Wood

Metal

Wood

We use these words to describe them:

- hard,
- stiff,
- firm,
- rigid,
- tough.

What hard materials can you find?

Changing shape

Materials can be shaped to make lots of things.

Soft materials
can be shaped
by hand.

Hard materials
can be shaped
with tools.

Clay play

We shape some materials
with a push or pull.

I've used clay to
make monster
models!

Clay

Metal foil

Paper

Metal spoon

Plastic scissors

Wood

Which of these things can you push or pull to change their shape?

Building towers

Rabbit built a tower.

It wobbled around.

Then it fell down.

Now Sam is helping Rabbit
to build a better tower.

13

House bricks

Bricks are shaped from soft clay.

They are fired to make them hard.

Bricks are used
to build houses.

What other materials
are used to build
houses?

How to...

Sometimes we follow instructions to shape and build.

Making this model was easy with instructions.

Build a mobile

Build a mobile using recycled materials.

Draw a picture of your mobile. Think about the materials you want to use.

Dionne pushes a pipe
cleaner through a straw.

Now she adds some more pipe cleaners.

Then she puts old CDs on the pipe cleaners.

What other recycled materials could you use?

4

Dionne puts beads on the ends of the pipe cleaners.

5 Finally it is ready to hang up.

21

Best paper plane

Follow these instructions to make the best paper plane ever!

1

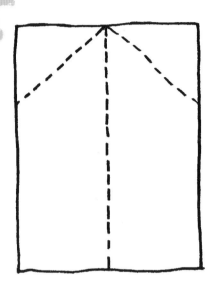

2

3

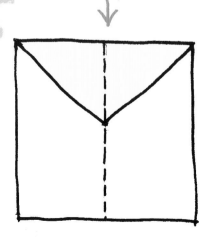

4

5

6

7

Try making it yourself first.

Ask for help if you get stuck.

Word picture bank

Bricks – P. 14, 15

Clay – P. 3, 10, 11, 14

Hard – P. 7, 9, 14

Instructions – P. 16

Model – P. 10, 17

Soft – P. 4, 9, 14, 15

First published in 2007 by Franklin Watts
338 Euston Road, London NW1 3BH

Franklin Watts Australia
Level 17/207 Kent Street, Sydney NSW 2000

Copyright © Franklin Watts 2007

Series editor: Adrian Cole
Photographer: Andy Crawford (unless otherwise credited)
Design: Sphere Design Associates
Art director: Jonathan Hair
Consultants: Prue Goodwin and Karina Law

A CIP catalogue record for this book is available
from the British Library.

ISBN: 978 0 7496 7617 9

Dewey Classification: 530.4

Acknowledgements:
The Publisher would like to thank Norrie Carr model agency.
'Rabbit' puppet used with kind permission from Ravensden PLC
(www.ravensden.co.uk).
Tiger Talk logo drawn by Kevin Hopgood.

Oscar Knott/Fogstock Alamy (14t).

Every attempt has been made to clear copyright.
Should there be any inadvertent omission
please apply to the publisher for rectification.

Printed in China

Franklin Watts is a division
of Hachette Children's Books,
an Hachette Livre
UK company.

There are 19 Tigers, including me, in this book. Did you find all of us?

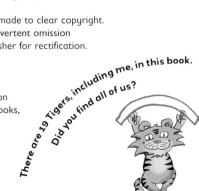